11+ Common Entrance Examination

Core subjects with mark schemes

Spring Term 2008

www.galorepark.co.uk

Supplied on behalf of ISEB by Galore Park Publishing Ltd
19/21 Sayers Lane, Tenterden, Kent TN30 6BW
www.galorepark.co.uk

© Independent Schools Examinations Board
Cover image: Ableimages

Typography by Typetechnique, London
Printed by Lego S.p.A Italy

ISBN: 978 0903627 80 1

All rights reserved: no part of this publication may be reproduced, stored in a retrieval system, or transmitted in any form or by any means, electronic, mechanical, photocopying, recording or otherwise, without either the prior written permission of the copyright owner or a licence permitting restricted copying issued by the Copyright Licensing Agency, 90 Tottenham Court Road, London W1P 0LP.

First published 2008

Details of other Galore Park publications are available at www.galorepark.co.uk

ISEB Revision Guides and publications may also be obtained from Galore Park.

Contents

Introduction iv

English Paper 1 1

English Paper 2 5

Mathematics 9

Science 25

Introduction

The examination papers in this booklet were set for the Spring Term 2008 Common Entrance Examination by the Independent Schools Examinations Board (ISEB). The syllabus for each subject is available from the ISEB website, www.iseb.co.uk. The book itself can be written in and suggested answers are provided in the accompanying mark scheme book. Other sessions and subject ranges are available to purchase from Galore Park, www.galorepark.co.uk

The copyright for this material belongs to the Independent Schools Examinations Board and photocopying is strictly forbidden without permission.

Independent Schools
Examinations Board

COMMON ENTRANCE EXAMINATION AT 11+

ENGLISH

PAPER 1

Monday 14 January 2008

Please read this information before the examination starts.

- You have 5 minutes' reading and planning time.
- After that you may start writing your answers when you are ready to do so. You have 40 minutes for writing.
- Answer in full sentences.
- Use your best handwriting and take care with spelling and punctuation.

Read the passage below and answer the questions which follow it.

A teenage girl called Ione is putting up posters in her village to advertise a jumble sale she has planned.

Ione walked across the road to the primary school. She had hoped it would be locked up still, for the holidays, and that she could just put her poster up on the gate without asking Miss Casterpool's permission. Ione had never cared for Miss Casterpool, and Miss Casterpool had never cared for her. But the tell-tale bottle-green mini was parked on the
5   kerb just outside, and the narrow side door was open. The summer holidays had clearly ended for the primary children. If Miss Casterpool was back today, they would be back tomorrow, and Ione herself would be next. Sighing, she walked across the tarmac playground and through the side door.

The sick feeling hit her at once, as she had known it would. For every time she returned, for
10 one reason or another, to these corridors and washrooms, classrooms and cloakrooms, she would hear noises and smell smells and see scratches in the woodwork that in all the six years she had spent at the school she had never even noticed, but which now she had left made her gasp with a sudden aching sense of renewed familiarity and of loss.

Ione now walked through the corridors, raising herself on her toes to peep through all the
15 small square glass panes set high in the doors, until she found Miss Casterpool in the infants' classroom, sorting flash cards. Ione remembered flash cards vividly. A rush of revulsion swept her other more delicate feelings away, and she shuddered slightly as she came through the door.

Miss Casterpool did not look up from the flash cards.

20 'Can I put this poster up on the playground gate?' Ione asked her politely.

'May I,' corrected Miss Casterpool, still not looking up.

Ione sighed. She found May-I grown-ups trying. It was, she recalled, one of the reasons she had never cared for Miss Casterpool.

'May I, then?' she asked.

25 'No,' said Miss Casterpool, beginning a new pile for short vowel sounds, 'you may not. The playground gates were not designed for posters.'

'It's a very worthy cause,' said Ione. 'It's to buy bullocks to pull ploughs to till the soil to plant seeds to grow food for hungry people. A very worthy cause,' she repeated.

'It would set a dangerous precedent,' warned Miss Casterpool, laying all the flash cards with
30 words ending in silent 'e' on one side.

'Dangerous?'

'All manner of people, seeing your poster on the playground gates, might come to me seeking permission to put up their own posters as well.'

'So?' said Ione.

35 Miss Casterpool looked up from the flash cards for the very first time. She studied Ione's face closely.

'Are you being insolent, Ione?' she asked. Not being sure whether she was or not, was, Miss Casterpool recalled, one of the reasons she had never cared for Ione.

'No, Miss Casterpool,' said Ione, falling back promptly on the dumb bland tone of voice she
40 knew from experience was the only one Miss Casterpool could take. 'I'm not, really.'

'The gate is not a notice-board,' said Miss Casterpool frostily. 'I consider the subject closed. And, Ione, please carry that other box of flash cards to the office for me on your way out.'

Ione stood perfectly still for a moment. She was willing every single part of her not to feel five years old again, or act that way. And as soon as she was sure she was quite ready, she
45 said calmly:

'No. No, I won't. It might set a dangerous precedent. All manner of people, seeing me carrying your flash card box to the office, might want to carry it too.'

She walked out. With immense self-control she pulled the door to behind her, as quietly as she could. Even if the Brownies put on *Frankenstein*, with real lightning, next year, they
50 would never get her inside the primary school again.

1. Why did Ione hope that the school would still be on holiday? (1)

2. Does the school strike you as old-fashioned? Give examples from the passage to support your view. (2)

3. What makes Ione sigh (line 7)? (2)

4. The flash cards play an important part in this passage.

    (a) What do these flash cards reveal about Miss Casterpool? (3)

    (b) How does Ione use the flash cards to get her own back on Miss Casterpool? (3)

5. The phrase 'had never cared for' is used several times (lines 3, 4, 23, 38). Why do you think the author repeats it? (4)

6. What do lines 27–28 reveal about Ione's character? (4)

7. This extract is told from Ione's viewpoint. Now write Miss Casterpool's version of this meeting in her diary entry that night. (6)

(Total marks: 25)

The passage is from *The Other Darker Ned* by Anne Fine, published by Teens Mandarin.

English Paper 1

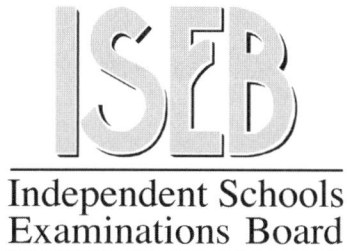

Independent Schools Examinations Board

COMMON ENTRANCE EXAMINATION AT 11+

ENGLISH

PAPER 2

Tuesday 15 January 2008

Please read this information before the examination starts.

- You have 5 minutes' reading and planning time.
- After that you may start writing when you are ready to do so. You have 40 minutes for writing.
- Use your best handwriting and take care with spelling and punctuation.

Write an essay using ONE of the following titles. Each one is worth 25 marks.

1. High Windows

2. Most of us know the feeling of 'It's not fair', to which grown-ups may reply, 'Well, life isn't fair!' Write about the last time *you* felt the need to cry, 'It's not fair!'

3. Choose one of the following titles to write about:

    (a) The Noah's Ark

    (b) Smoke

    (c) Silence

4. Which historical event are you most sorry to have missed? Write a vivid account of it, bringing out why it is so significant to you. You can write as if you were there, if you want to.

5. Have you read a book containing a character you would love to be? Write in detail about that character, bringing out the differences and similarities between the two of you.

6. Write in any way you like about the picture opposite.

(Total marks: 35, including a mark out of 10 for spelling/syntax/punctuation)

SURNAME .... FIRST NAME ....

JUNIOR SCHOOL .... SENIOR SCHOOL ....

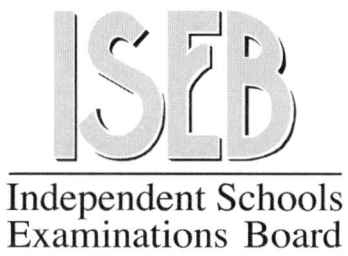

COMMON ENTRANCE EXAMINATION AT 11+

MATHEMATICS

Monday 14 January 2008

Please read this information before the examination starts.

- This examination is 60 minutes long.
- Please try **all** the questions.
- Write your answers on the dotted lines.
- All working should be written on the paper.
- Tracing paper may be used.
- Calculators are not allowed.

Mathematics

1. Pat collects stamps.

   She has 144 British stamps and 68 foreign stamps.

   (i) How many stamps does she have in total?

   Answer: .... (2)

   (ii) How many more British stamps than foreign stamps does she have?

   Answer: .... (2)

   (iii) Pat arranges her 144 British stamps in an album. Each page holds 6 stamps. How many pages does she use?

   Answer: .... (2)

   (iv) Her brother, Lee, has 3 times as many foreign stamps as she does. How many foreign stamps does he have?

   Answer: .... (2)

2. (a) Write down the number which is 10 more than 291

   Answer: .... (1)

   (b) Write down the number which is 10 less than 1108

   Answer: .... (1)

   (c) Write down the number which is 100 times bigger than 40

   Answer: .... (1)

   (d) Write down the number which is 10 times smaller than 83

   Answer: .... (1)

   (e) The temperature in a fridge is 2 °C.
   The temperature in the freezer is 10 °C colder.
   What is the temperature in the freezer?

   Answer: .... °C (2)

Mathematics

3. Here is the start of a number pattern:

2   3   5   8   13   21   34   55   89

From the numbers above, write down

(i) a multiple of 4

Answer: .... (1)

(ii) a prime number bigger than 6

Answer: .... (1)

(iii) two numbers with a difference of 18

Answer: .... and .... (1)

(iv) two numbers whose product is 26

Answer: .... and .... (1)

(v) the median of the nine numbers

Answer: .... (2)

4. Notby School won the final of the hockey tournament.

   (i) A hockey pitch is 91.4 metres long.
   Write this length in centimetres.

   Answer: .... cm (1)

   (ii) There were 2096 spectators at their final match.
   Write this number correct to the nearest hundred.

   Answer: .... (1)

   (iii) The hockey trophy weighed half a kilogram.
   How many grams is this?

   Answer: .... g (1)

   Mr Gowl, the hockey coach, carried out a survey to see whether the children who scored goals were right-handed or left-handed.

   Here are his results in a Venn diagram:

   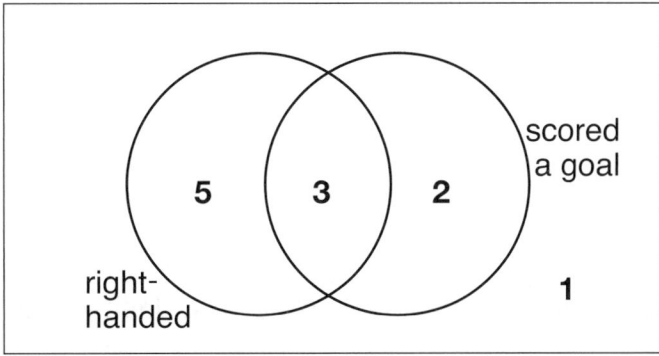

   (iv) Use the Venn diagram to write down

   (a) the number of right-handed children in the team

   Answer: .... (1)

   (b) the number of left-handed children who scored a goal

   Answer: .... (1)

Mathematics 13

5. (i) Plot the following points on the centimetre grid below:
   (2, 2) (6, 2) (4, 4)
   (The first one has already been done for you.) (2)

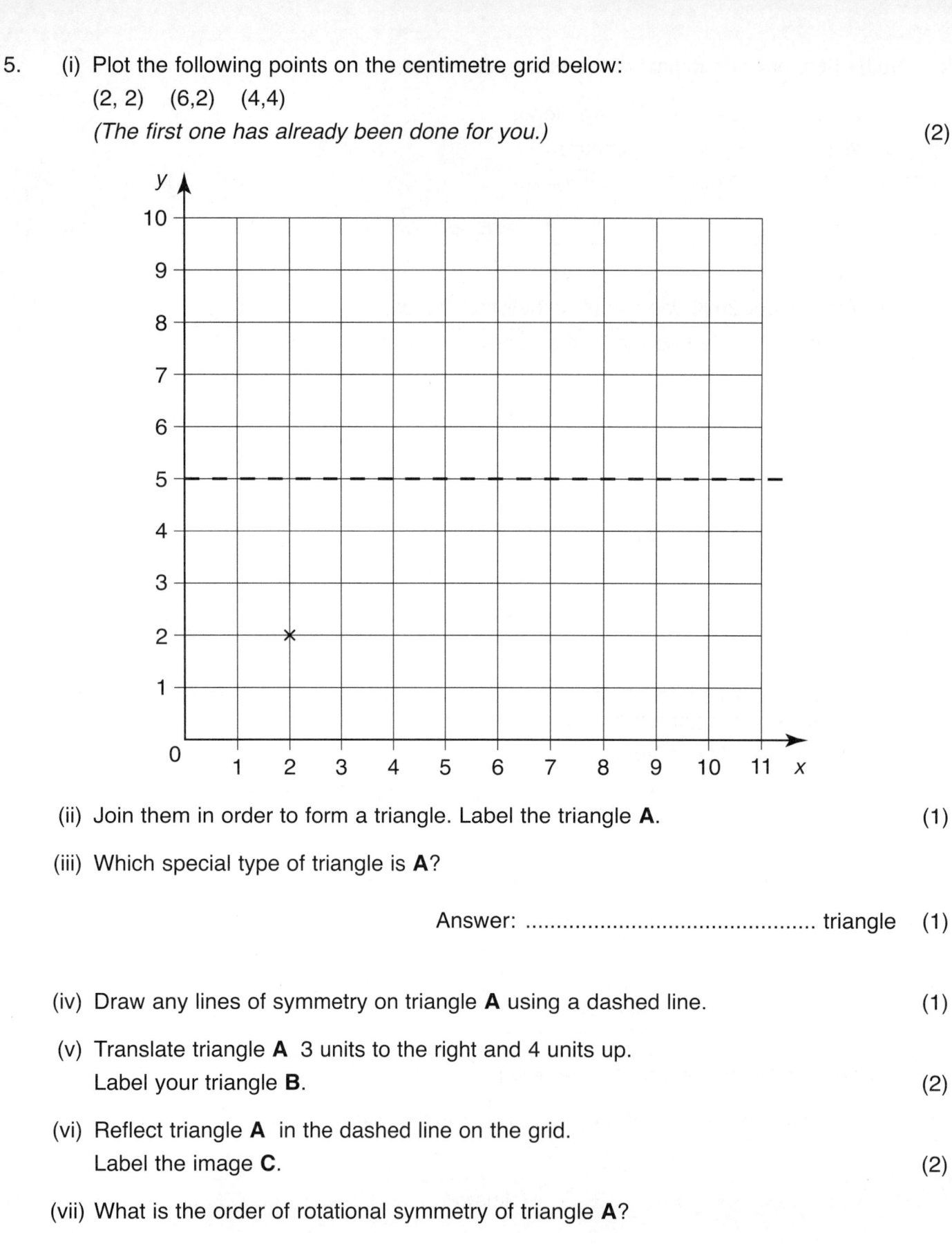

(ii) Join them in order to form a triangle. Label the triangle **A**. (1)

(iii) Which special type of triangle is **A**?

Answer: .... triangle (1)

(iv) Draw any lines of symmetry on triangle **A** using a dashed line. (1)

(v) Translate triangle **A** 3 units to the right and 4 units up.
   Label your triangle **B**. (2)

(vi) Reflect triangle **A** in the dashed line on the grid.
   Label the image **C**. (2)

(vii) What is the order of rotational symmetry of triangle **A**?

Answer: .... (1)

(viii) Find the area of triangle **A**.

Answer: .... cm² (1)

6. Five teams took part in the relay race at sports day.

   Here are their results:

team name	time taken to finish, in seconds	position
Active Eight	51.2	......
Cheetahs	48.34	1st
Speedy Sports	51.08	......
Twisters	59.9	5th
X-treme	50.8	......

   (i) Complete the table to show their positions. (2)

   (ii) How much faster was the team which came first than the team which came fifth?

   Answer: .... s (2)

   The team Cheetahs broke the school record by 1.9 seconds.

   (iii) What was the previous school record?

   Answer: .... s (2)

   Active Eight had 4 runners in their team.

   (iv) Find the mean time for each runner in this team by dividing their total time by 4

   Answer: .... s (2)

Mathematics 15

7. Robert asked all the children in his school on which day of the week they were born. Here is a bar chart showing his results:

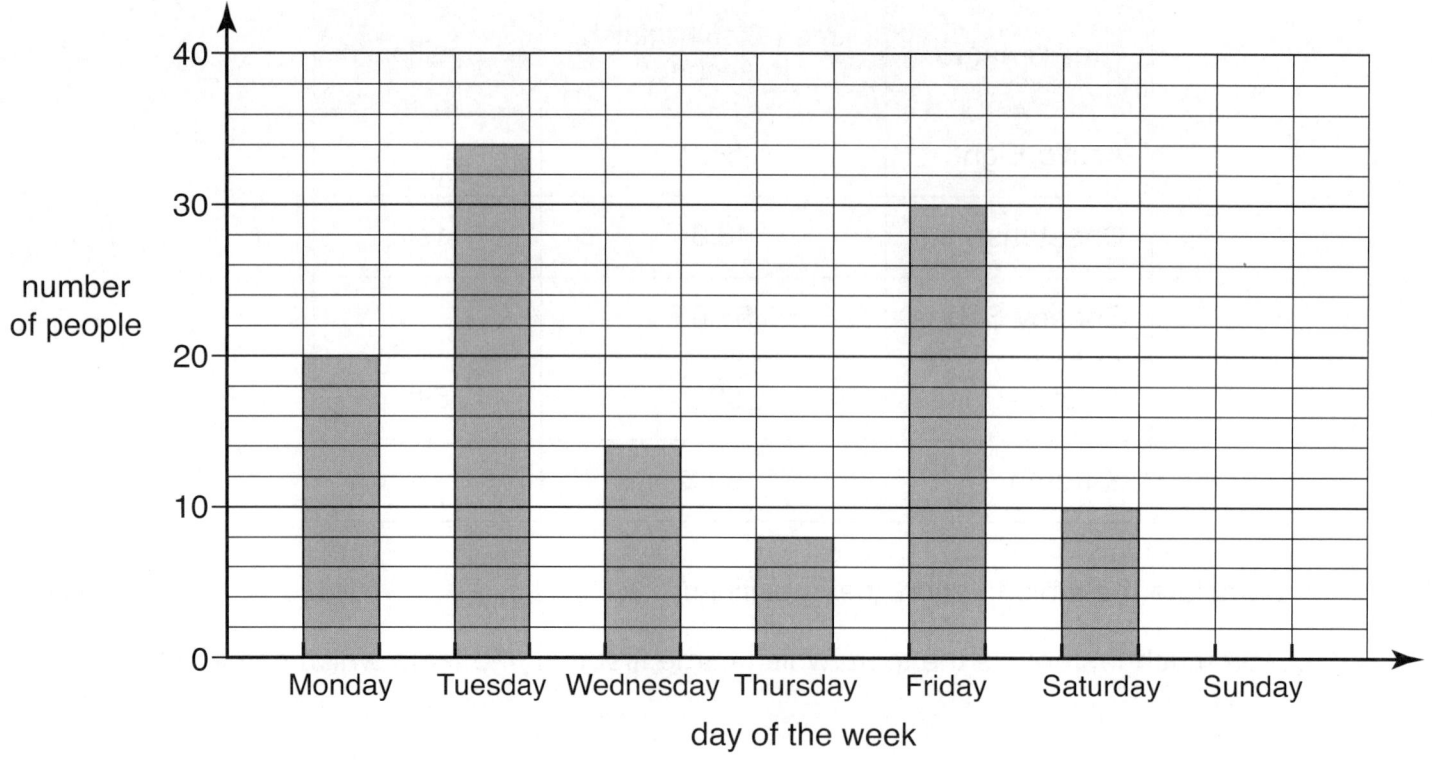

(i) How many people does each small rectangle represent?

Answer: .... (1)

There were 22 people born on Sunday.

(ii) Draw a bar on the chart to represent this. (1)

(iii) Use the bar chart to complete the frequency table below.

day of the week	number of people
Monday	
Tuesday	
Wednesday	14
Thursday	
Friday	
Saturday	10
Sunday	22

(2)

(iv) Which day is the mode?

Answer: .... (1)

8. Katherine has ten coins in a bag.

She has one 50-pence coin, two 20-pence coins, one 5-pence coin and the rest are 2-pence coins.

(i) What is the total value of all the coins in her bag?

Answer: £ .... (3)

(ii) What percentage of the coins are 20-pence coins?

Answer: .... % (1)

(iii) One coin is picked at random from the purse.
On the scale below, mark

(a) with **A** the probability that the coin is a 20-pence coin (1)

(b) with **B** the probability that the coin is not a 20-pence coin (1)

(c) with **C** the probability that the coin is worth less than £1 (1)

impossible   certain

Mathematics

9. Here are the ingredients needed to make a tray of 20 flapjacks:

   200 grams of margarine
   250 grams of oats
   200 grams of sugar
   100 grams of flour
   3 tablespoons of syrup

   (i) Write out the ingredients you would need to make 10 flapjacks.

   .... grams of margarine

   .... grams of oats

   .... grams of sugar

   .... grams of flour

   .... tablespoons of syrup (3)

   Kelly needs to make 50 flapjacks for a party.
   (ii) How much flour does she need?

   Answer: .... grams (2)

   To make healthier flapjacks, you can use $\frac{3}{4}$ of the recommended amount of sugar.
   (iii) How much sugar would you use to make 20 of these healthier flapjacks?

   Answer: .... grams (2)

10. Alan climbs to the top of a mountain one day during his holiday.

Below is a graph showing his height above sea level at different times during the day.

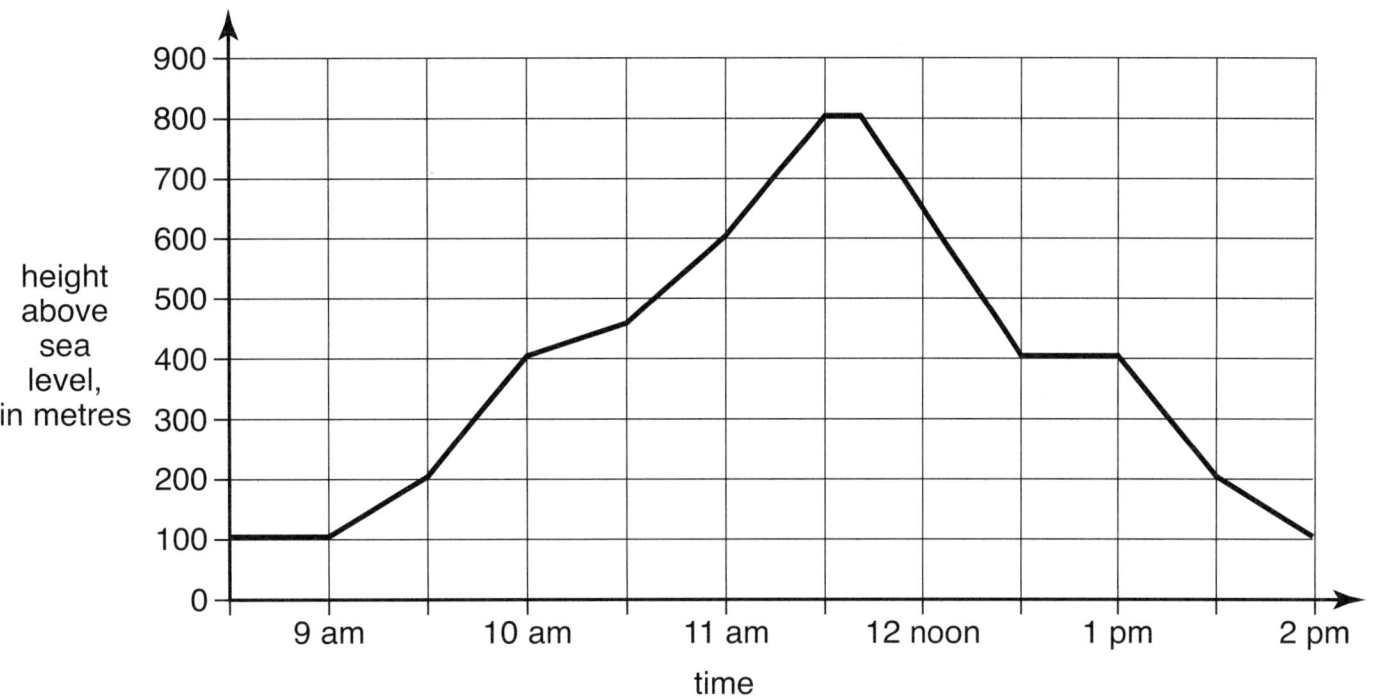

(i) How many metres above sea level is he at 11 am?

Answer: .... m   (1)

(ii) At what time does he first reach 200 metres above sea level?

Answer: ....   (1)

(iii) How many metres above sea level is the top of the mountain?

Answer: .... m   (1)

(iv) (a) Between which times does he stop on the way down?

Answer: .... and ....   (2)

(b) Give a sensible suggestion for why he might have stopped at this time.

Answer: ....   (1)

11. Adam's father has hidden Adam's birthday present in a field near their house.

    He has given him these instructions to help him find it.

    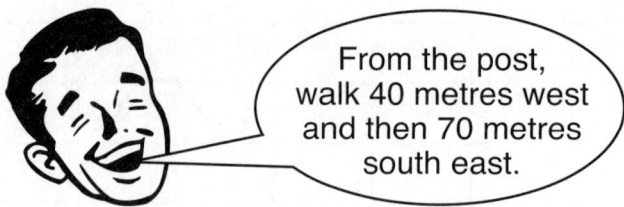

    From the post, walk 40 metres west and then 70 metres south east.

    Adam has decided to draw an accurate map to help.

    (i) Using a scale of 1 millimetre to represent 1 metre, draw accurately the route which Adam's father has described.

    You will need to use a protractor.

    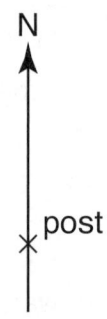

    (3)

    (ii) Adam realises that it will be shorter to walk in a straight line to find his present.

    (a) Draw this route on your diagram. (1)

    (b) Write down the length of this route in centimetres.

    Answer: .... cm (1)

    (c) How far does this represent in the field?

    Answer: .... m (1)

12. Bert and Chrissy are very good at maths and enjoy 'think of a number problems'.

    Bert asks Chrissy to think of a number, double it and add 5

    She says that the result is 33

    (i) What was the number she thought of?

    Answer: .... (2)

    Chrissy wants Bert to guess her favourite number.

    She asks him to write down 5 numbers.

    He chooses   **4   7   2   19**   and   **8**

    Chrissy looks at the numbers and tells him that her favourite number is equal to the mean of the numbers, minus 7

    (ii) Find the mean of Bert's numbers.

    Answer: .... (3)

    (iii) What is Chrissy's favourite number?

    Answer: .... (1)

    (iv) Circle any of the words below which describe Chrissy's favourite number.

    prime number   **square number**   **cube number**   (2)

13. Farmer Fred needs to build a rectangular sheep pen.

   To save money, he decides to build it against his barn, so that he only needs to have fencing on three sides.

   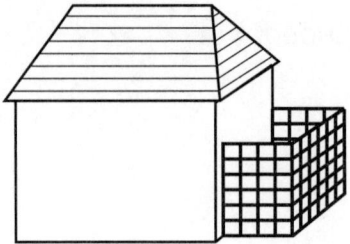

   Here is the first plan:

   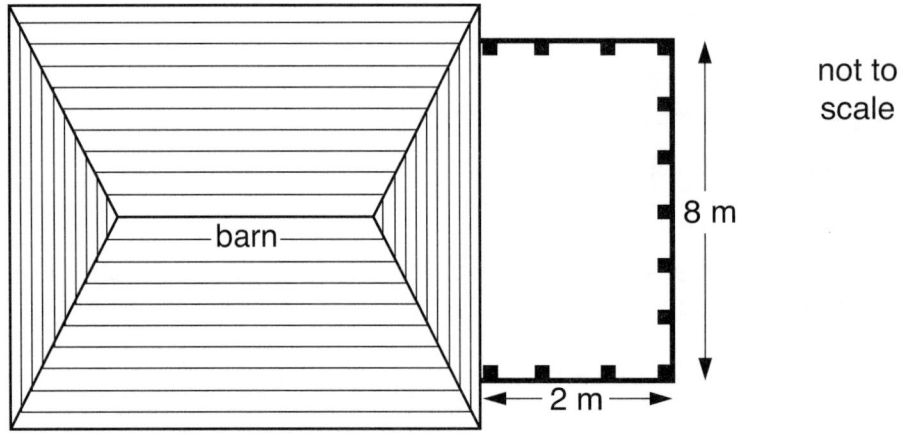

   (i) (a) What length of fence does he need to make this pen?

   Answer: .... m (1)

   (b) What is the area of this pen?

   Answer: .... m² (1)

   He decides to buy 15 metres of fence.
   Here is his new plan:

   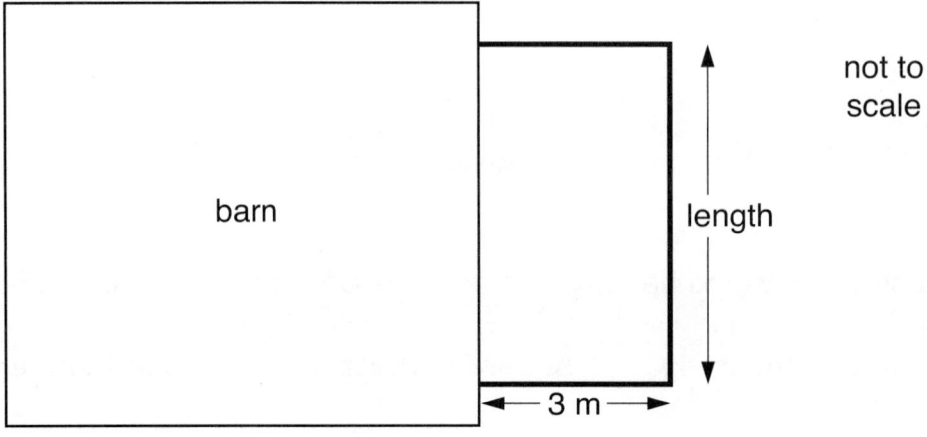

(ii) Find the length of his new pen.

Answer: .... m   (1)

Farmer Fred decides that he would like to build a square pen with his 15 metres of fence as shown below:

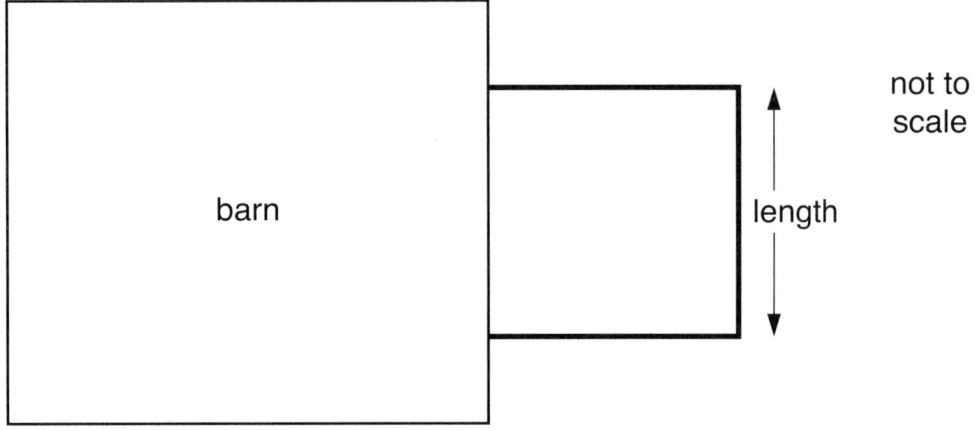

(iii) How long should each side be?

Answer: .... m   (2)

(iv) Given that 1 metre of fence costs £12, find how much it will cost Farmer Fred to buy 15 metres of fence.

Answer: £ ....   (3)

14. Look carefully at these number patterns:

	pattern A			pattern B
row 1	$1^2 - 0^2$ →	$1 - 0$ →	1	$1 + 0 = 1$
row 2	$2^2 - 1^2$ →	$4 - 1$ →	3	$2 + 1 = 3$
row 3	$3^2 - 2^2$ →	$9 - 4$ →	5	$3 + 2 = 5$
row 4	$4^2 - 3^2$ →	$16 - 9$ →	7	$4 + 3 = 7$

(i) Complete rows 5 and 6 of this pattern:

| row 5 | $5^2 - 4^2$ → | $25 - .....$ → | 9 | $5 + ... = ...$ |
| row 6 | $6^2 - .....$ → | $..... - .....$ → | ..... | $..... + ... = ...$ |

(3)

(ii) Complete row 10 of this pattern:

| row 10 | $..... - .....$ → | $..... - .....$ → | ..... | $..... + ... = ...$ |

(2)

(iii) Complete the non-shaded parts of these rows:

| row 20 | $..... - .....$ → | $..... - 361$ → | ..... | $..... + ... = ...$ |
| row ..... | $..... - 99^2$ → | $..... - .....$ → | ..... | $..... + ... = ...$ |

(3)

(iv) What is the value of $1000^2 - 999^2$?

Answer: .... (1)

(Total marks: 100)

SURNAME .... FIRST NAME ....

JUNIOR SCHOOL .... SENIOR SCHOOL ....

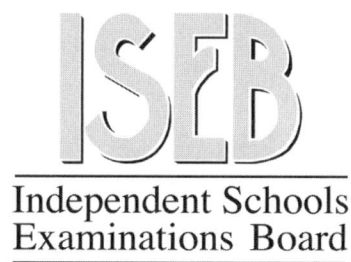

Independent Schools
Examinations Board

COMMON ENTRANCE EXAMINATION AT 11+

SCIENCE

Tuesday 15 January 2008

Please read this information before the examination starts.

- This examination is 60 minutes long.
- Answers are to be written on the question paper.
- Answer **all** the questions.
- You are allowed to use a calculator.

Science

25

© ISEB 2008

1. Here is a diagram of the Sun, the Earth and the Moon.

not to scale

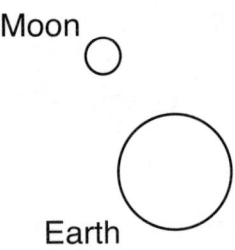
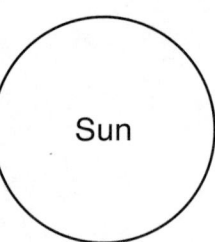

(a) Shade the section of the Earth which is in darkness. (1)

(b) The Moon orbits the Earth. How long does it take for one orbit?

.... (1)

(c) What is the approximate shape of the Moon?

.... (1)

2. (a) A teacher carefully placed a beaker over a burning candle.

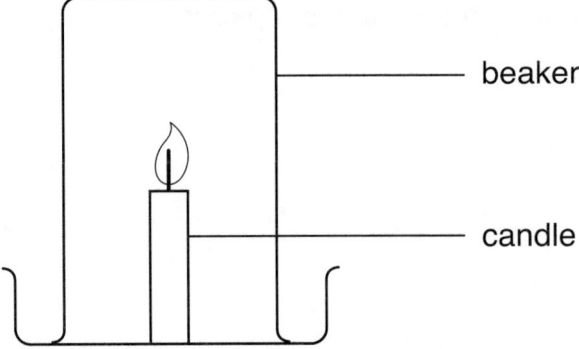

The class observed that after a short time the candle went out and a black substance and a colourless liquid were found on the inside of the beaker.

(i) Is this a reversible or a non-reversible change?

.... (1)

(ii) Give a reason for your answer.

.... (1)

(b) Candle wax can be formed from a fossil fuel.

(i) Explain the meaning of the term *fossil fuel*.

....

.... (1)

(ii) Give an example of a liquid fossil fuel used in cars.

.... (1)

(iii) Give an example of a liquid fossil fuel used to heat a house.

.... (1)

(iv) Gaseous fuels are also sometimes used for heating. In the boxes below, show how the particles are arranged in a liquid and a gas.

liquid	gas

(2)

Science 27

3. The picture below shows a tawny owl.

(a) The owl is a *nocturnal* bird. It is a fierce *predator* and eats mainly small mammals. Explain what these two words mean.

nocturnal: .... (1)

predator: .... (1)

(b) Some features of the owl are labelled on the diagram. Suggest one way in which each of these helps this nocturnal hunter to obtain and eat its food.

large, forward-facing eyes: ....

....

sharp claws: ....

....

strong, sharp beak: ....

.... (3)

(c) Tawny owls eat frogs, small birds, small mammals (e.g. field mice and voles), insects and worms. Field mice and voles eat seeds.

In the space below, write a food chain which includes the tawny owl.

(3)

(d) Owls cannot digest the bones of their prey. In the owl's stomach, the bones are made into a pellet and then brought back up to the mouth. These pellets are found on the ground below the owl's roosting place. It is possible to tell what the owl has been eating by breaking sterilized pellets open and looking at the bones.

Here are the results of a study of the pellets produced by one owl in one day.

pellet	mammals	birds	others
1	2 voles 1 field mouse	1 bluetit	1 frog 1 beetle
2	1 vole	none	2 beetles
3	1 field mouse 1 house mouse	1 hedge sparrow	none

Complete the bar chart below to show the result of the survey of the owl's diet for one day.

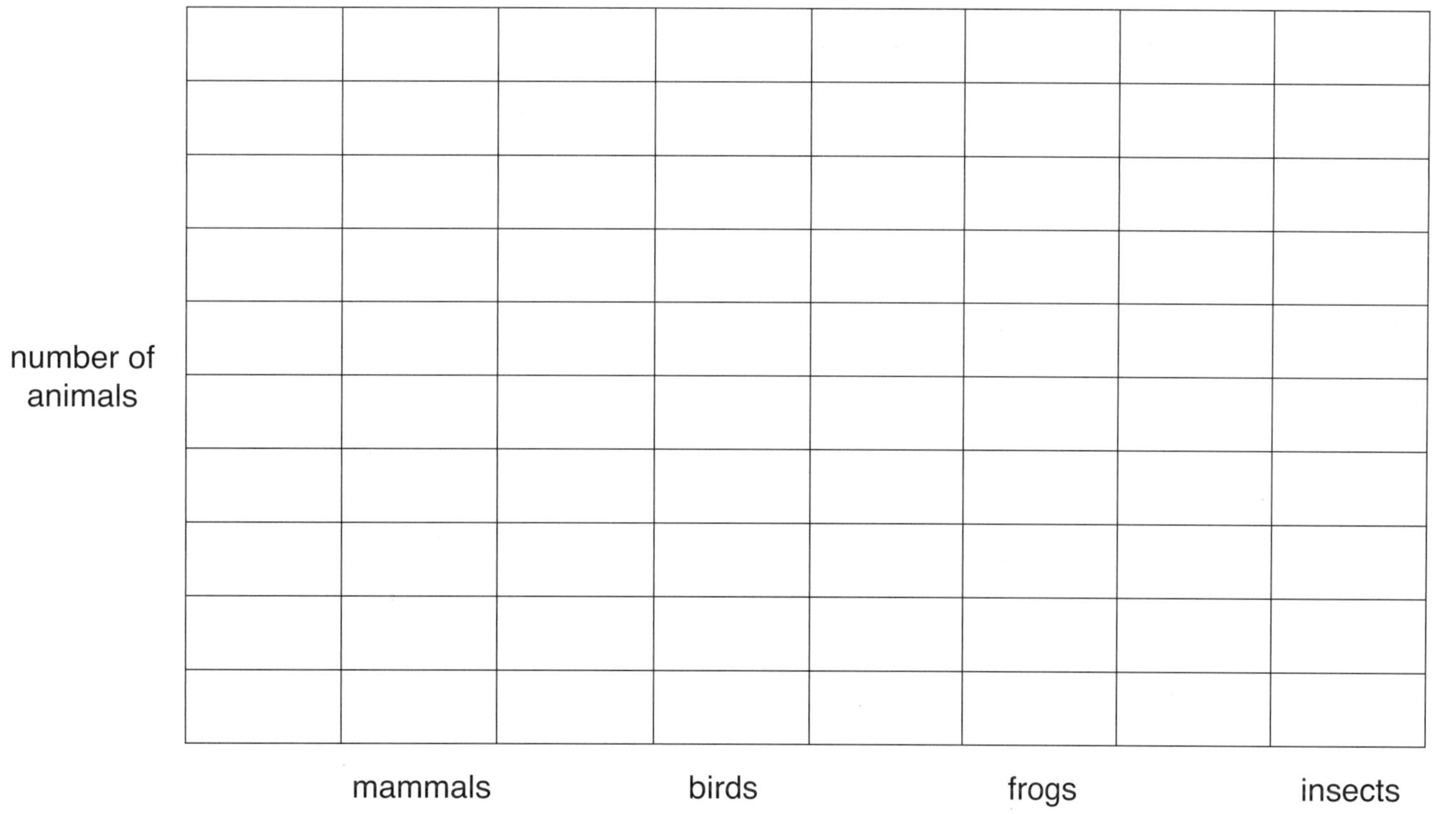

number of animals

mammals   birds   frogs   insects

(4)

4. Chris is a musician and plays many different instruments.

   (a) Here is his xylophone.

   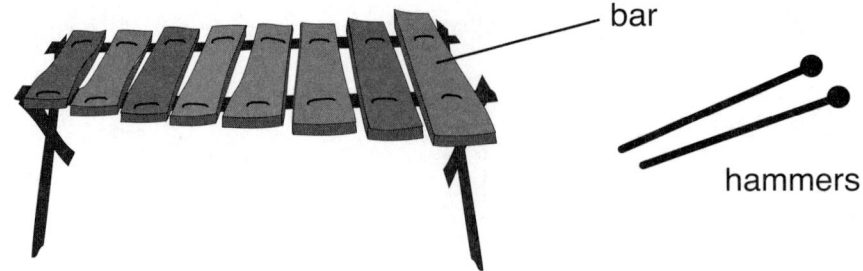

   (i) Explain why a sound is made when Chris hits the bars with the hammers.

   ....

   .... (2)

   (ii) If Chris hits the shortest bar and then the longest bar equally hard, what difference in the sounds would he hear?

   ....

   .... (2)

   (b) Chris plays some large drums. Here is a picture of one of them.

   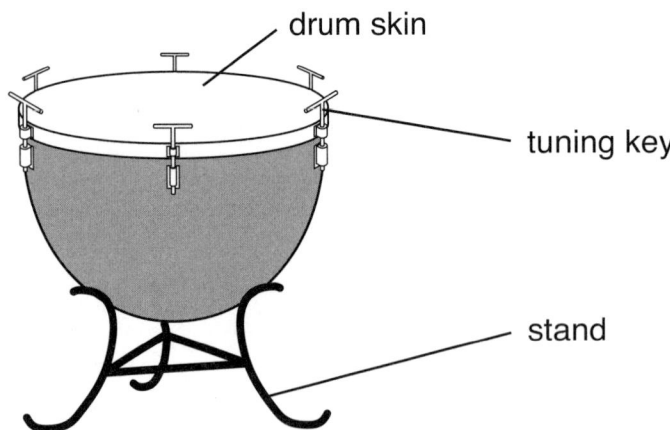

   (i) In a rehearsal, the conductor asked Chris to make a quieter sound on his drums. How will Chris change the way he plays the drum to make the sound quieter?

   .... (1)

(ii) Chris makes the drum skin tighter with the tuning keys. How will the sound change?

.... (1)

(c) Complete the following sentence:

Sound travels through solids, liquids and ...., but not

through a .... (2)

5. Kate sketched the circuit she had designed to see if a motor turned.

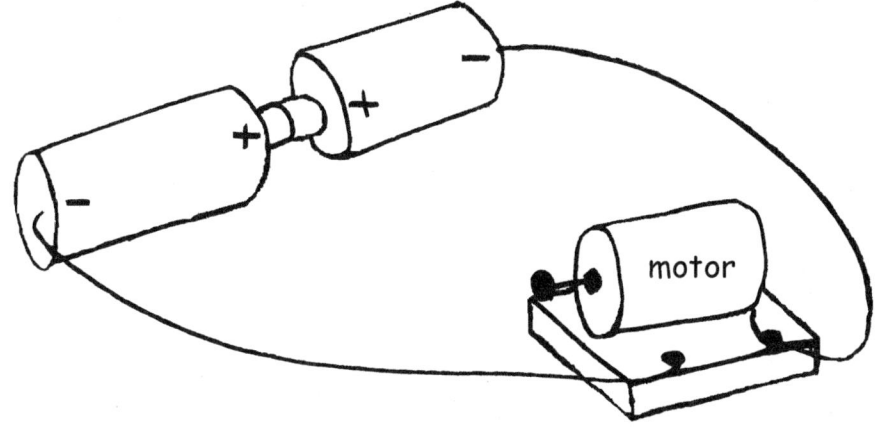

(a) She then built the circuit and found that the motor did not work. Explain why.

....

.... (1)

(b) Kate corrected her circuit and added a switch. Draw a circuit diagram of this circuit. Use the correct circuit symbols.

(4)

6. Pupils were asked to separate a mixture of salt and pepper.

    (a) Peter put some of the mixture into a beaker and added some warm water and stirred. One of the solids dissolved and one did not.

        (i) Which solid dissolved?

        .... (1)

        (ii) Which word describes a substance which does not dissolve?

        .... (1)

        (iii) Why did Peter stir the mixture?

        .... (1)

        (iv) Give one safety precaution Peter should take when carrying out this experiment.

        .... (1)

    (b) Peter then filtered the mixture.

        (i) Which solid was left on the filter paper?

        .... (1)

        (ii) Which scientific word is used for the substance which is left on the filter paper?

        .... (1)

    (c) Peter left the filtrate in a beaker on a window sill and after a few days a solid was left.

        (i) Which substance had evaporated?

        .... (1)

        (ii) Give two ways in which Peter could make this substance evaporate more quickly.

        1: ....

        2: .... (2)

7. (a) The diagram shows a flower which has been cut in half.

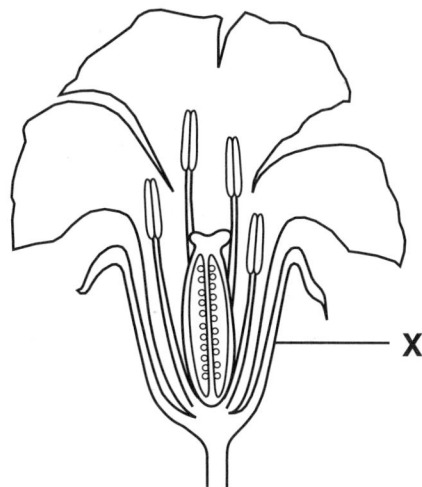

(i) What is the name of part **X**?

.... (1)

(ii) What is the function of part **X**?

.... (1)

(b) Select the best word from the following list to fill each of the spaces in the passage below. *(Each word may be used once, more than once or not at all.)*

anthers	dispersed	fertilization
fruits	ovules	petals
pollination	style	stigma

In flowering plants, pollen is produced by the .... The transfer of pollen to a .... is known as .... Later, seeds are formed inside the ovaries. The ovaries develop into .... After the seeds have been .... , they may germinate and grow into plants.

(5)

8. Simon was training for his school's sports day. He ran round his local park ten times every day.

   Simon's bones and muscles enable him to move. Some of these are shown in the picture below.

   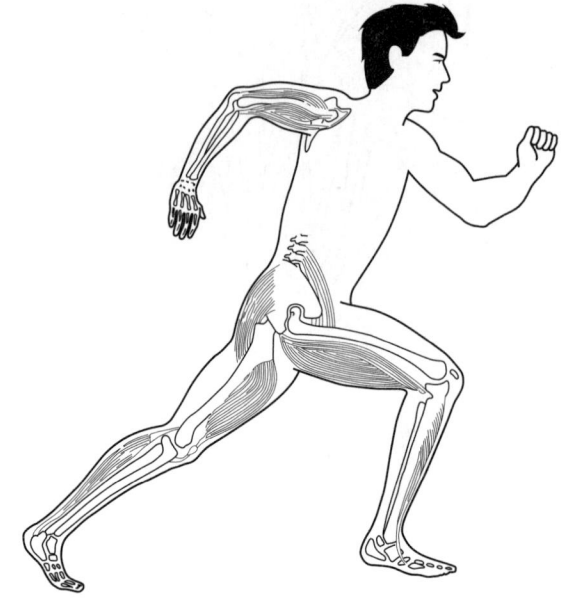

   (a) (i) Label a muscle with the letter **M**. (1)

   (ii) Label a bone with the letter **B**. (1)

   (iii) Describe how muscles cause movement of the skeleton.

   .... (1)

   (b) Another function of the bones in our bodies is to protect vital organs.

   (i) Name a part of the skeleton which does this.

   .... (1)

   (ii) What does this part protect?

   .... (1)

(c) (i) Which name is given to animals with internal skeletons?

.... (1)

(ii) Give two examples of these.

1: ....

2: .... (2)

(d) Exercise helps us to keep healthy. What is one benefit of exercise?

.... (1)

9. Megan and Kevin wanted to grow healthy radish plants. They knew that the seeds would need a soil which drained well, but not too quickly. They set up an experiment to test three different types of soil to decide which would be the best for their seeds to germinate. They poured 50 cm³ of water onto the different soils and measured the volume of water which passed through after five minutes.

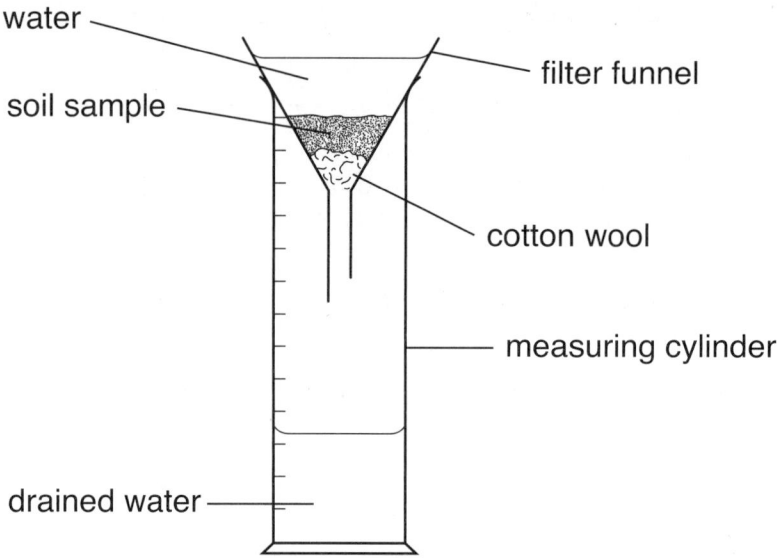

Their table of results is shown below.

trial	volume of water, in cm³ which passed through in 5 minutes		
	soil A	soil B	soil C
1st try	48	30	11
2nd try	47	28	10
3rd try	49	20	10
4th try	48	32	13
mean (average)	48		

(a) (i) One result in the table should be ignored. Circle it. (1)

(ii) Suggest how this result could have happened.

.... (1)

(b) Calculate the mean (average) for soils B and C, leaving out your circled result. Write your answers in the table above. (2)

(c) (i) Which soil, A, B or C, do you think had the largest particles?

.... (1)

(ii) Is this soil likely to be loam, clay or sand? .... (1)

(d) (i) Which soil, A, B or C, would you predict would be the best for Megan and Kevin to grow their seeds in?

.... (1)

(ii) Explain why the other two soils are less suitable.

....

.... (2)

(e) State three conditions which will be needed for the successful germination of their radish seeds in the chosen soil.

1: ....

2: ....

3: .... (3)

Science 37

10. Ben wanted to find which surface provided the most grip to run on to practise sport. He used a training shoe to test the following surfaces:

          carpet   **tarmac**   **wood**

(a) Describe how he could carry out a fair test to investigate which surface provided the most grip.

....

....

....

....

....

....

....

....

You may use this space to draw a diagram.

(4)

(b) What should he do to check the reliability of his results?

....

.... (2)

(c) Explain how he will decide which surface provides the most grip.

.... (1)

(d) Suggest what he could do to extend his investigation.

....

.... (1)

(Total marks: 80)

Science 39